THE STIN

A Three Part Healing Process To Freedom

Nicole Taylor

Table of Contents

Acknowledgments

I would like to thank my Heavenly Father for giving me the grace to complete this book.

He has given me the insight, grace and language to get this project done. I would like to thank Him for His keeping power where my house didn't lack any good thing while I was writing. I was still able to homeschool my children, attend to my house and be present with my husband when he needed my attention. I thank Him for such ease when it comes to my responsibility. God has been the sustaining force for leading me through the healing from the sting of betrayal. He has given me the tools to overcome, the insight to heal and the strategies to move into freedom. I am forever grateful to have such a loving Father to help me and love on me through this process. I pray this book will heal and help you, as much as it did me.

Let's journey with Him.

Introduction

" How art thou fallen from heaven, O Lucifer, son of the morning! how art thou cut down to the ground, which didst weaken the nations! For thou hast said in thine heart, I will ascend into heaven, I will exalt my throne above the stars of God: I will sit also upon the mount of the congregation, in the sides of the north: I will ascend above the heights of the clouds; I will be like the most High. Yet thou shalt be brought down to hell, to the sides of the pit." (Isaiah 14:12-15 KJV)

"And there was war in heaven: Michael and his angels fought against the dragon; and the dragon fought and his angels, And prevailed not; neither was their place found any more in heaven. And the great dragon was cast out, that old serpent, called the Devil, and Satan, which deceiveth the whole world: he was cast out into the earth, and his angels were cast out with him. And I heard a loud voice saying in heaven, Now is come salvation, and strength, and the kingdom of our God, and the power of his Christ: for the accuser of our brethren is cast down, which accused them before our

God day and night. And they overcame him by the blood of the Lamb, and by the word of their testimony; and they loved not their lives unto the death. Therefore rejoice, ye heavens, and ye that dwell in them. Woe to the inhabiters of the earth and of the sea! for the devil is come down unto you, having great wrath, because he knoweth that he hath but a short time." (Revelation 12:7-12 KJV)

"Moreover the word of the Lord came unto me, saying, Son of man, take up a lamentation upon the king of Tyre, and say unto him, Thus saith the Lord God; Thou sealest up the sum, full of wisdom, and perfect in beauty. Thou hast been in Eden the garden of God; every precious stone was thy covering, the sardius, the topaz, and the diamond, the beryl, the onyx, and the jasper, the sapphire, the emerald, and the carbuncle, and gold: the workmanship of thy tabrets and of thy pipes was prepared in thee in the day that thou wast created. Thou art the anointed cherub that covereth; and I have set thee so: thou wast upon the holy mountain of God; thou hast walked up and down in the midst of the stones of fire. Thou wast perfect in thy ways from the day that thou wast created, till iniquity was found in thee. By the multitude of thy merchandise they have filled the midst of thee with violence, and thou hast sinned: therefore, I will cast thee as profane out of the mountain of God: and I will destroy thee, O covering cherub, from the midst of the stones of fire. Thine heart was lifted up because of thy beauty, thou hast corrupted thy wisdom by reason of thy brightness: I will cast thee to the ground, I will lay thee before kings, that they may behold thee. Thou hast defiled thy sanctuaries by the multitude of thine iniquities, by the iniquity of thy traffick; therefore, will I bring forth a fire from the midst of thee, it shall devour thee, and I will bring thee to ashes upon the earth in the sight of all them that behold thee." (Ezekiel 28:11-18 KJV)

We all have experienced betrayal or have betrayed someone in life. No matter what took place, the outcome of betrayal is always hurt and disappointment. We look at the one that has betrayed us or even ourselves as the enemy, but really, it's the spirit of Lucifer that has used us or them to betray. This book is intended to help those of you who have been affected by the sting of betrayal or have been the betrayer. I will take you through a step by step process to show you how to break free from the walls you've created, teach you how to forgive yourself and others, help you to renew your mind and restore your hope to receive healthy relationships. I'll also show you how to get unstuck to move beyond the acts betrayal. You'll go through a transformation process that will challenge you to be the new creature that God has created you to be. You'll receive all the resources you need from Heaven to move forward freely.

The first betrayal took place in Heaven with God and Lucifer. Lucifer was known as the son of the morning. He was so beautiful and glorious that he had stones radiating from his body. He was known as the being that sang so beautifully and worked right next to God. I'm sure God was very disappointed when Lucifer tried to exalt himself above Him. Lucifer developed iniquity in his heart to do such a wicked thing, that's why God had to send His judgement on him and cast him down.

God cannot have such wickedness in His Kingdom, because it contaminates His world. He did not want sin and evil reigning in His midst. Everything He created and built was good and was beautiful. I believe He intended for His Kingdom to be pure and Holy to bring forth life to those that reside there. It was a place of paradise that provided peace and rest for all who were there.

Betrayal can only take place when someone is close to you. Someone that you trust and share you life and secrets with. The relationship will start out right in the beginning but in the midst of the journey they switch on you. The spirit of Lucifer will hijack the mind, expectations and intentions of people to have them turn on you. I think that's when iniquity flourishes in the hearts of those that will end up betraying you. "But every man is tempted, when he is drawn away of his own lust, and enticed. Then when lust hath conceived, it bringeth forth sin: and sin, when it is finished, bringeth forth death." (James 1:14-15 KJV)

It takes the wickedness of iniquity to defile someone's heart to betray you. They end up violating the right they have with you and use it against you. They look for ways to overtake you and dethrone you from your position. The jealousy in them is a driving force to undermine you and shut you down. It is all fueled by hatred and the devil himself.

Now that Lucifer was cast down, he was known as the first orphan that was rejected by the Father. He tries to release that same orphan tendencies to the minds of the God's people so that they will not come into the true knowledge of God. He wants to keep you separated from God, just like he deceived Adam and Eve in the Garden of Eden. He wanted to recruit them to disobey God to destroy their lives. Sad to say, they fell for it. "Now the serpent was more subtil than any beast of the field which the Lord God had made. And he said unto the woman,

Yea, hath God said, Ye shall not eat of every tree of the garden? And the woman said unto the serpent, We may eat of the fruit of the trees of the garden: But of the fruit of the tree which is in the midst of the garden, God hath said, Ye shall not eat of it, neither shall ye touch it, lest ye die. And the serpent said unto the woman, Ye shall not surely die: For God doth know that in the day ye eat thereof, then your eyes shall be opened, and ye shall be as gods, knowing good and evil. And when the woman saw that the tree was good for food, and that it was pleasant to the eyes, and a tree to be desired to make one wise, she took of the fruit thereof, and did eat, and gave also unto her husband with her; and he did eat. And the eyes of them both were opened, and they knew that they were naked; and they sewed fig leaves together, and made themselves aprons. And they heard the voice of the Lord God walking in the garden in the cool of the day: and Adam and his wife hid themselves from the presence of the Lord God amongst the trees of the garden. And the Lord God called unto Adam, and said unto him, Where art thou? And he said, I heard thy voice in the garden, and I was afraid, because I was naked; and I hid myself. And he said, Who told thee that thou wast naked? Hast thou eaten of the tree, whereof I commanded thee that thou shouldest not eat? And the man said, The woman whom thou gavest to be with me, she gave me of the tree, and I did eat. And the Lord God said unto the woman, What is this that thou hast done? And the woman said, The serpent beguiled me, and I did eat. And the Lord God said unto the serpent, Because thou hast done this, thou art cursed above all cattle, and above every beast of the field; upon thy belly shalt thou go, and dust shalt thou eat all the days of thy life: And I will put enmity between thee and the woman, and between thy seed and her seed; it shall bruise thy head, and thou shalt bruise his heel. Unto the woman he said, I will greatly multiply thy sorrow and thy conception; in sorrow thou shalt bring forth children; and thy desire shall be to thy husband, and he shall rule over thee. And unto Adam he said, Because thou hast hearkened unto the voice of thy wife, and hast eaten of the tree, of which I commanded thee, saying, Thou shalt not eat of it: cursed is the ground for thy sake; in sorrow shalt thou eat of it all the days of thy life; Thorns also and thistles shall it bring forth to thee; and thou shalt eat the herb of the field; In the sweat of thy face shalt thou eat bread, till thou return unto the ground; for out of it wast thou taken: for dust thou art, and unto dust shalt thou return. And Adam called his wife's name Eve; because she was the mother of all living. Unto Adam also and to his wife did the Lord God make coats of skins, and clothed them. And the Lord God said, Behold, the man is become as one of us, to know good and evil: and now, lest he put forth his hand, and take also of the tree of life, and eat, and live forever: Therefore, the Lord God sent him forth from the garden of Eden, to till the ground from whence he was taken. So, he drove out the man; and he placed at the east of the garden of Eden Cherubims, and a flaming sword which turned every way, to keep the way of the tree of life." (Genesis 3:1-24 KJV)

In the midst of the betrayal, God had a plan that will cancel out all the corruption that Satan planned to bring into the earth. And that was Jesus! He sent His Son to destroy sin and bring the people back into relationship with Him. Jesus is ALWAYS the answer to healing when it comes to betrayal. Satan wanted the betrayal to get you out of covenant with the Father, but I pray that the sting of betrayal will cause you to run to the Father to restore your relationship with Him.

PART 1

The Sting of Betrayal in Relationships

The Sting Of Betrayal In Friendship

The Frenemy

" And lest I should be exalted above measure through the abundance of the revelations, there was given to me a thorn in the flesh, the messenger of Satan to buffet me, lest I should be exalted above measure. For this thing I besought the

Lord thrice, that it might depart from me. And he said unto me, My grace is sufficient for thee: for my strength is made perfect in weakness. Most gladly therefore will I rather glory in my infirmities, that the power of Christ may rest upon me." (2 Corinthians 12:7-9 KJV)

"For it was not an enemy that reproached me; then I could have borne it: neither was it he that hated me that did magnify himself against me; then I would have hid myself from him: But it was thou, a man mine equal, my guide, and mine acquaintance. We took sweet counsel together, and walked unto the house of God in company." (Psalms 55:12-14 KJV)

"For I have heard the whispering and defaming words of many, "Terror on every side! Denounce him! Let us denounce him!" All my familiar and trusted friends, [Those who are] watching for my fall, say, "Perhaps he will be persuaded and deceived; then we will overcome him, And take our revenge on him." But the Lord is with me as a dread champion [one to be greatly feared]; Therefore, my persecutors will stumble and not overcome [me]. They will be completely shamed, for they have not acted wisely and have failed [in their schemes]; Their eternal dishonor will never be forgotten. But, O Lord of hosts, You who examine the righteous, Who see the heart and the mind, Let me see Your vengeance on them; For to You I have committed my cause." (Jeremiah 20:10-12 AMP)

"He also that received seed among the thorns is he that heareth the word; and the care of this world, and the deceitfulness of riches, choke the word, and he becometh unfruitful." (Matthew 13:22 KJV)

We know that betrayal by a close friend is devastating. The sting is real. How do we think Jesus feels when we run the risk of cultivating a compromised heart? When we do that, we betray Him, because our hearts are not committed to being consistent and stable in believing that He is the Son of God. We see that with Judas in (John 13:21-26). Jesus reveals that Judas heart was not with Him, even though He chose him to be His disciple. (John 6:70-71) I believe that Jesus chose Judas to buffer Him to prove that God's grace is sufficient. It's the same thing that Paul went through in (2 Corinthians 12:7-9) "And lest I should be exalted above measure through the abundance of the revelations, there was given to me a thorn in the flesh, the messenger of Satan to buffet me, lest I should be exalted above measure. For this thing I besought the Lord thrice, that it might depart from me. And he said unto me, My grace is sufficient for thee: for my strength is made perfect in weakness. Most gladly therefore will I rather glory in my infirmities, that the power of Christ may rest upon me."

When someone betrays you, they turn you over to your enemy for their selfish desires to crucify you. They don't truly believe that God sent you or that you're being used by God. They become a unbeliever at heart even though they've walked with you and saw the power of God at work in your life. Peter denied Jesus out of fear. Judas betrayed Jesus because He didn't believe in Him even though He saw all the miracles, healing, deliverance and raising people from the dead.

Where there is secrecy there is betrayal. Judas made his plans secretly and tried to take the money back but ended up committing suicide because they didn't accept it. The enemy will use you, then condemn you and kill you. Judas went out with Jesus, but he didn't follow Him. He understood what Jesus was saying, but he didn't accept it. (1 John 2:19) Judas' life stands as a solemn warning to us — a warning against the dangers of hypocrisy and unbelief. Don't let the sting of betrayal inject its venom into you and cause you to become offended, bitter, unforgiving and revengeful.

Even in the extremity of betrayal by a friend, revenge is counterproductive. You end up setting yourself up to fall into a trap. You think you're hurting the person that hurt you but really, you're bringing destruction on your life. It's important to let go of the pain, so God can heal you and cause you to bless those that have betrayed you. They meant it for evil against you, but God meant it for your good.

God wants to take your pain to purify you and have you come out as pure gold. Your purity will be a testimony of God's goodness in keeping you whole in the midst of the pain. The sting was there to buffet you and cause you to humble yourself in the midst of the hurt. God wants to prove that His grace is sufficient for you, His strength is made perfect in your weakness and that the cares of this world will not choke you out by the thorn sting of betrayal.

The Sting of Betrayal in Mentorship

The Mentally ILL Mentor and The Honorable Mentee

We see in 1 Samuel 18 that Saul became jealous because he didn't think that David would overcome the Philistines. The thing that seemed to put Saul over the edge was the song of victory by the women that Saul had killed his thousands, but David his ten thousand. David was able to kill ten thousands because he had God with him to fight the battle. Two can put ten thousands to flight. (Deuteronomy 32:30) There's great victory when you fight your battles with God.

Saul as a mentor to David for kingship, he didn't think that God would exalt David over him. He believed that he can still stay in position while he disobeyed God. He didn't realize that God already fired him and hired David for the position. Saul's disobedience opened him up to a evil spirit that God sent to torment him. It reminds me of Matthew 18:34-35 where the Lord will turn you over to the tormentors if you don't forgive your brother.

You see, Saul had unforgiveness in his heart towards himself for disobeying God and he thought that he could get away with it. He didn't think that God would hold him accountable for not dealing with the Amalekites. Saul's unforgiveness turned into bitterness and hatred for the one that God has chosen to be king. Disobedience can open the door for you to become a betrayer. When you see someone that is close to you obeying God and doing the very thing that God has called YOU to do, it can cause you to be envious.

Envy flourishes in the shade of another's glory. It will cause you to diminish the person that God has exalted and try to exalt yourself over them and God. You end up stealing God's glory and parading yourself to receive the praise from men. He will not share his glory with another. (Isaiah 42:8) The Lord brings down the proud but He gives grace to the humble. I believe the Lord fired Saul not just because of his disobedience but also because of his pride and lack of trust in God. He trusted in his own strength and ability to lead God's people.

You really have to be deceived to think that you can still work for God while being disobedient. Saul struggled with a evil spirit that tormented him and caused him to be mentally ill. He was tossed to and fro in his thinking pattern to love David one minute and then looking to kill him the next. Saul was mentally unstable so much so that he tried to recruit people to plot against David to kill him.

Envy will cause you to have mental issues and make you revengeful against the one that God had chosen to deliver you. David played the harp to ease Saul's mind from being tormented. David still honored Saul in the midst of Saul trying to kill him. *"And the men of David said unto him, Behold the day of which the Lord said unto thee, Behold, I will deliver thine enemy into thine hand, that thou mayest do to him as it shall seem good unto thee. Then David arose, and cut off the skirt of Saul's robe privily. And it came to pass afterward, that David's heart smote him, because he had cut off Saul's skirt. And he said unto his men, The Lord forbid that I should do this thing unto my master, the Lord's anointed, to stretch forth mine hand against him, seeing he is the anointed of the Lord." (1 Samuel 24:4-6 KJV)*

Saul knew that God was with David and he still looked for opportunities to kill him. You really have to be possessed by the enemy to launch an attack against God's chosen king. David was wise because even though he had an opportunity to kill Saul, he didn't do it because he didn't want to go against God's chosen one.

David exemplified the character that Saul should've had.

And God sent that evil spirit on him. In Deuteronomy 28:27-29 it is the Lord that will smite you with madness, blindness and bewilderment of heart just by being disobedient. We all can learn from this. Being a leader, mentor or overseer in any capacity, it's important to obey God in everything.

Don't allow your position to validate the pride in you. Don't allow all that you have built, trained or started to be exalted over the plan of God for your life. Don't allow it to cause you to disobey God and miss out on the blessings He has for you. Don't allow envy to crowd your heart and cause you to minimize what God has placed on someone else's life.

Envy will cause you to always have a negative response to the accomplishments of others. Be careful how you treat those that you mentor, oversee and lead, you may feel like they're not qualified for the position, but God can fire you and hire them. Ask Saul. (1 Samuel 16:1-13)

Learning from David is the best way to stay clear from the spirit of envy, hatred, unforgiveness and betrayal. David lived a life that pleased God. He was honorable, humble, loyal and committed to Saul even in the midst of him trying to kill David. Jesus did the same thing with Judas, he served him, loved on him and kept Judas close to him. Wherever your treasure is there where your heart be also. (Matthew 6:21) Jesus's heart was with Judas even when Judas betrayed him. Remember Judas was the treasurer. Let your heart still be with those that have betrayed you. Let's model Jesus's example in believing that we can still bless, love and restore those that have hated you.

The Sting of Betrayal in A Romantic Relationship

The Deceptive Seductress

Samson was dedicated to the Lord at birth. His family consecrated him for the Lord's service. They told him not to get mixed up with the Philistines because he was called to deliver the people out of their hands. Samson trusted his own strength in disobeying the instructions of his parents and the Lord. (Judges 13)

Samson was courageous before men but weak when it came to women. He got caught up in a romantic relationship that later destroyed his life. He didn't think that making this mistake would alter his destiny and cause him to go into another direction. He got distracted and led by the lust of the flesh, the lust of the eyes and the pride of life. (1 John 2:15-17)

Delilah was his downfall, his enemy and his trap. She ensnared him with false compassion, false comfort and false affection. Her seduction was his deception and his secret was her answer. She was hired to destroy his life and prepare him for death. (Judges 16)

She manipulated, provoked and bewitched him to give her the secret to his strength. The secret to Samson's strength was the 7 locks of his hair. When Samson kept this information to himself, he was able to defeat, conquer and overtake his enemies. But after he revealed his secret, he lost his strength.

The sting of betrayal took place before he even noticed it. He went into this situation spiritually blinded and didn't discern that he was resting his head, thought patterns and mindset in the lap of a witch. He was already battling psychological warfare because he was vexed in his soul unto death when she kept provoking him for answers.

She pulled on his heart strings and released mind control to get what she wanted. He was blinded by her seductions and bewitched by her words until he was desensitized. He was numb to the red flags, warnings and cautions of the Holy Spirit. She was on a witch hunt for his spiritual sight, spiritual strength and spiritual life.

The Lord departed from Samson when he gave her the secret. He didn't have supernatural strength to fight his enemies while he was sleeping with the enemy. He lost all power, might and strength. They chained him up, gouge out his eyes and locked him away. He was bound.

I believe the Philistines were just manifesting what was already taking place in the spirit. Samson was already chained up mentally, bound by her love and locked away from fulfilling destiny. While he was locked away he repented before the Lord and asked Him to give him strength one more time so he can overcome them.

God in His loving kindness and mercy granted his request. He gave him back supernatural strength and power to destroy the philistines and everyone else who was around. I believe Samson died after that because he was able to complete his assignment and fulfill his calling which was to deliver the people from the hand of the Philistines.

This story is to reveal to you that even in the sting of betrayal in a romantic relationship, God still has purpose for your life. When you repent for entertaining a relationship that has defiled you, He'll still use you for his glory and fulfill destiny. Samson was recognized in the faith hall of fame (Hebrews 11) because of his repentance and obedience at the last stage of death. Most of the men and women of God that are recognized didn't live perfect lives but their heart was to obey God. Your name can be written in the lambs book of life through repentance.

God is not looking for perfection, He is looking for repentance and obedience. He wants you to be recognized in Heaven and on earth for living a life that pleased Him. He's looking to rewrite your story, and use it, so others can have courage in walking with Him. Be His living epistle.

The Sting of Betrayal In Family

The Dreamer and The Curse Of Familiarity

The sting of betrayal in family can be disheartening, because you believe that family is there to have your back in life. It's sad to say, that sometimes that's not always the case. Family can be your downfall if you're not careful. As we look at the story of Joseph, we see how family can try to destroy your destiny. (Joseph 37)

We see that Jacob loved Joseph the youngest son more than his brothers. Living in that kind of environment can create a lot of tension with jealousy and sibling rivalry through favoritism. Jacob being the Father created that mess because he didn't love his children equally. How many of us have seen that in our own families? It seems like the parent or caretaker will have a special love for a particular child and dismiss the others.

That's a dangerous way to build a family, but I also know that it's not always easy to share your love equally with your children. That's why we need to ask the Lord to show us how to love and see our children His way. Jacob loved Joseph so much that he gave him a tunic of many colors. I believe Jacob was blessing his son with a mantle of impact for every tribe, nation and tongue.

It seems as though, Jacob already knew that Joseph was going to be a great leader one day but he didn't think that Joseph would end up leading him. It shows that Jacob wasn't humble enough to receive his son (the youngest) to lead him because he was his father. Parents have to be careful to not allow pride to rule them and reject the call that God has placed on their children's lives. Even Jesus had to save His mother (Mary) when He died on the cross and that was His calling. She had to be humble enough to receive the salvation of her son. (John 19:25-30)

Joseph brothers hated him because of the multicolor tunic. They hated him even more when he shared his dream with them. They didn't feel like Joseph was qualified to rule over them because of his age. I love what Paul tells Timothy as a Spiritual Father- Don't let people despise your youth. (1 Timothy 4:12) Many times people can despise you because of your age and the favor that God has placed on your life. They can also despise you because of familiarity.

Family positioning can sometimes mean that you unwillingly take the posture of a household or indentured servant. Family members see you as a means to serve them, to be at their beck and call, and respect what THEY want for you. Familiarity can cause family members, friends and people to dishonor you because they feel like they know you intimately, have seen your flaws and believe that you are not qualified to do anything great.

Joseph's brothers knew he was going to reign over them and have rulership. Their hatred, envy and evil against their brother increased. They were fueled by the spirit of Cain to plot against Joseph instead of being their brother's keeper. They believed that if they killed Joseph it would stop the dream from coming to pass.

The brothers stripped Joseph of his mantle of many colors but didn't realize that his calling lived on the inside of him and not on the coat. Sometimes family will try to strip you of your giftings, talents and callings, if you don't use it to serve them. They will try to bury you alive and cover up the greatness that's on the inside of you. This is why Joseph brothers dropped him in the pit.

When they saw the Ishmaelites they pulled Joseph out of the pit to sell him into slavery. They sold him for 20 shekels of silver not knowing that they were paying their way into poverty. The betrayal took place, because Reuben didn't know that his brothers took Joseph out and sold him. He went to tear Joseph's tunic, slaughter a male goat and dipped it in blood to send to Jacob. The brothers still didn't tell Reuben that they sold him. They not only betrayed Joseph but they also betrayed Reuben so they can keep the money for themselves.

Out of Reuben's ignorance he created a covenant with death by dipping Joseph's tunic in the goats blood. The spirit of death behind that altar had Reuben to believe that Joseph was dead and to carry that news back to Jacob. Unfortunately, Jacob didn't know the story was false. Favoritism started the journey, jealousy carried out its assignment and the spirit of death was SUPPOSED to be the end result.

But I love how God perseveres the life of those that He wants to use for His glory. No matter how much they hate you, betray you, bury you, diminish you, discount you, forget you, reject you and sold you, know that Jesus already paid the price and bought you.

You see, Joseph thought that was the end of him, but God was preparing him for promotion and leadership to rule over those that have hurt him. In the midst of it, Joseph had to be mature in helping his family when they didn't have any resource in the famine. Joseph had to forgive those that have despitefully used him and did evil against him. Know that your enemies cannot prevail against you when God has favored you!

PART 2

Healing Betrayal – Dysfunctional to Functional Relationships

N ow that we have looked at the dysfunction in relationships, let's look at what is healthy. I believe the first part of healing the wounds of betrayal, is to look at healthy relationships to shift your mind and restore your hope. God can give you healthy relationships that can fuel you, but first you've got to become healthy yourself. There is no use in expecting healthy relationships if you have not dealt with the hurt, trauma and disappointments of your heart. In this 3 part healing process, I will begin to show you how to get healed from the sting of betrayal, master heart issues and identity healthy relationships.

Dysfunctional to Functional Friendship

Judas and Jesus to Jonathan and David Friendship

Let's look at the first betrayal. Judas and Jesus. This was a friendship relationship. Judas betrayed Jesus, but Jesus still loved him and died on the cross for him. In friendship, it may seem like it's hard to love the one that has come against you. We see that it's not hard at all, because Love is a choice and Jesus decided to love regardless of the hurt. Jesus made up his mind to lay down his life for his friend to prove that His love for Judas was great. (John 15:13) You cannot say that you love God and hate your brother. You will be considered a liar in the eyes of God.

Here are 8 steps to get healed from the sting of betrayal in friendship.

1. Acknowledge the sting/hurt

2. Ask God to reveal how you have betrayed your friend in the relationship?

3. Confess those faults to Him

4. Repent

5. Ask Him for forgive you

6. Confront the issue head on, by contacting that person and discussing the issue

7. Forgive yourself, God and the person

8. Release them in Love and truly LET IT GO!

These steps can help you master the issues in your heart, because you will have to face the bitterness, offence, hurt, disappointment, resentment and the sting that has caused you to not love and trust again. When you do that, God will begin heal you where you hurt, shift your mind from those painful memories and restore your hope for healthy relationship.

As you work on your heart, change your view and ask God to purge you. He will show you the condition of your heart. It's important to know if your heart is ready to embrace a healthy relationship. You don't want to step into a relationship prematurely if you have not dealt with the sting, because you will sabotage and forfeit the purpose of the relationship. Be honest with yourself, because it takes courage to love again, hope again and trust again. It will not be fair to start a friendship if you know you're not ready to lay down your life for them.

Let's look at one of the ways you will be able to identify a healthy friendship.

We see in 1 Samuel 18:1-4 that Jonathan's soul was knit to David and he loved him. That was a brotherhood that could not be broken. Their friendship stood the test of time that Johnathan revealed to David that his father, Saul, had planned to kill him. The love they had for one another was healthy that Jonathan was able to strip off his armor to give to David. Jonathan left himself uncovered to cover his friend for battle. I believe Jonathan got a revelation that David needs to be equipped for the journey ahead and Jonathan had the tools to give to him to fulfill the will of God on his life.

1. A healthy friend will see what God is doing through you and prepare you to be obedient to the call. (1 Samuel 18:4)

2. A healthy friend will tell you when they see the enemy coming to attack you, pray with you, give you wisdom on what to do and admonish you to stay hidden in the secret place before God. (1 Samuel 19:2)

3. A healthy friend will speak for you and defend you when your enemy is trying to accuse you. (1 Samuel 19:4-7)

Those are just some of the qualities you will find in a healthy friend, there are many more ways you can identify a healthy friend. We also have to make sure that when we find these qualities in friendship that we can give those same qualities to them in return. Friendship is not one sided, you have to give and reciprocate love as well. You will have to be healthy in your heart, renewed in your mind, whole in your soul and refreshed in your spirit to have a healthy friendship.

Dysfunctional to Functional Mentorship

Saul and David to Paul and Timothy Mentorship

When it comes to a mentorship relationship, we have to ask God to heal us from those that we have trusted to guide us. We see that Saul as a mentor/leader got jealous of David, but David still honored him.

Here are 8 steps to get healed from the sting of betrayal in mentorship

1. Acknowledge the disappointment
2. Still honor them even when they have hurt you
3. Pray for them
4. Ask God to heal you
5. Ask God to heal them- hurt people, hurt people
6. Forgive them
7. Bless them as you exit the relationship
8. Set boundaries

Mastering heart issues can be difficult in this situation, because you have not done anything wrong for them to treat you the way they did. But they have done something wrong to you and that can affect you spiritually, emotionally and mentally. When someone in leadership has the ability to guide, aid, oversee and lead you and they have abused their authority over you, there is an oppression that takes place to feel like your obligated to still submit, serve and obey their commands. That is unhealthy, because spiritually your being suppressed, mentally your being controlled and emotionally your being hurt. All of that can distort and change your view and perspective on God and even leadership. That's why it's important to pluck up all the evil that they have done to sin against you so that it won't affect you.

Now let's look at what a healthy relationship in mentorship looks like.

We see in Acts 16:3 that Paul circumcised Timothy which is symbolic of his covenant he made with him as a mentor. Their relationship developed over time as Timothy traveled with Paul to learn all that he was going to pour into him. Paul as a spiritual father considered Timothy as a son in the faith. He imparted the spirit of Christ in Timothy as he was authentic in his own walk with the Lord. Paul was ready to hand the baton to Timothy because he was spiritually mature in his young age.

1. A healthy mentor is someone that will circumcise your heart to prepare you for leadership (Acts 16:3)

2. A healthy mentor is someone that will lead you to Christ as you follow them (1 Corinthian 11:1)

3. A healthy mentor is someone that will pour into you, equip you and push you as they pass the baton for you to run your race. (2 Timothy 4:1-7)

Be ready, be humble and position yourself to be mentored by someone that is healthy and wants to lead you into your destiny. Allow God to reveal Himself to you in the relationship and let that compel you to pursue Him more. If you're still dealing with the hurt of mentorship from the previous mentor, then be honest with the new mentor so they can help you, pray for you and encourage you to trust again. When they are sent by God, They are ready to work alongside you as Holy Spirit leads them. Most importantly, be obedient to God and the mentor He has placed in your life. Do not let them feel like it's a burden to oversee you. (Hebrews 13:17)

Dysfunctional to Functional Romance

Samson and Delilah to Priscilla and Aquila Romantic Relationship

In a romantic relationship it's hard to get over the sting of betrayal, because this is someone that you've shared your heart with. You fell in love with them and thought that they were in love with you, but they just wanted to use you. This took place with Samson. He got tangled up with Delilah and that altered the course of his life. When you choose to be in a relationship with someone that has intentionally hurt you, you have to seek out help and guidance. This is where you will have to get inner healing and deliverance from the soul tie that was created between the two of you.

Here are 8 steps to get healed from the sting of betrayal in romantic relationship

1. Repent
2. Seek out for inner healing
3. Go through deliverance
4. Cut soul ties
5. Release them
6. End the relationship
7. Do not go back to them

8. Understand your value

To master heart issues in this situation, you have to search your heart and ask God what is it in you that attracts that kind of person? Look within and find out what has caused you to be driven by your own lust and desire. Sometimes we entertain certain relationships, because we don't understand our worth and value. We compromise to be accepted and loved by the person that doesn't even care for us. We've been in dysfunction for so long that we consider it the norm. It has become our normal and we become desensitized to the Holy Spirit that we can't discern His warnings and red flags. In order to recognize something healthy we need to detox and purge our soul from the things that have contaminated us. That purging should take place in our mind, will, emotions and intellect.

Now, let's look at a healthy romantic relationship.

We see in Acts 18:2-3, a married couple Priscilla and Aquila had a healthy relationship. They exemplified a love for each other that was recorded and known in the bible. They worked together in ministry and helped those around them. They were known as tent makers, housing the people of God with love, care and hospitality. They have such a unity in everything that they did. They were a "power couple" advancing the Kingdom of God together. Their marriage glorified Christ and the Church.

1. A healthy romantic relationship will challenge you to be obedient to God, not derail you from Him.

2. A healthy romantic relationship will have the heart to serve God with you.

3. A healthy romantic relationship will want to honor God in everything that you do.

When it's time for you to entertain a romantic relationship, choose wisely. Get counsel, there is safety in it. You don't want to invest time, energy and money into someone that is not looking to do the will of God with you. Know your worth, identity and value. Get around healthy couples so you can have a reference point of what Kingdom relationship looks like. Learn from them and most importantly, be led by Holy Spirit when it comes to choosing someone to be apart of your life.

Dysfunctional to Functional Family

<u>Joseph and his family to Jesus and the Father Family Relationship</u>

We learned that Joseph went through a lot with his family. Family issues can affect you in such a deep way that you will create walls to stay away from them and have them stay away from you. Building walls is not the answer. Don't isolate yourself because of feeling hurt, rejected and disappointed of them. The Lord puts the lonely in family. I believe that's one of the tools in healing. Community. When you surround yourself with healthy people that are willing to accept you for you, flaws and all, healing can take place. You wouldn't have to perform for the approval of others. You can just be, because Christ already accepted you.

Here are 8 steps to healing from the sting of betrayal in family.

1. Forgive them
2. Place your heart before the Lord to heal you
3. Trust again
4. Believe again
5. Release them

6. Respect them
7. Set healthy boundaries with them
8. Love them

To mastering the heart issues in your family you will have to acknowledge the hurt. Don't be revengeful in trying to hurt them back. Place your offence, bitterness, hurt and rejection before the Lord. They don't owe you anything. Pull the walls down and believe that the Lord will cover you. Ask God to change your view about them and see them through His eyes, so you know how to love them His way. When you forgive you don't have to be reconciled to them. Forgiveness and reconciliation are two different things. You can still honor them even if you're not reconciled to them.

Let's look at a healthy family relationship.

We see that in the Kingdom of Heaven, when one accepts salvation they are grafted in as a son and daughter to the Father, through Jesus. They become a part of the family of God. Jesus lets us know that his family are those who hear the word of God and do it. (Luke 8:21) Jesus also questions the people and said who is my mother and father? Whoever does the will of the Father are His family. (Matthew 12:46-50) So we see that family is not necessarily blood, but those that are obedient to the Father are considered family. The same goes for you. When you get around a healthy church community that becomes your family. You share in the same interest in following after Christ. You function as a body jointly fit together as Christ being the head to go and save those that are lost.

1. A healthy family will give you identity, purpose and discover your destiny

2. A healthy family will love you for you, but will challenge you to become better

3. A healthy family will lead you to Jesus, so He can introduce you to your Heavenly Father.

Ask Holy Spirit to lead you to your tribe and family, so you can understand your DNA as a son and daughter, heir of God and joint heir with Christ. You're no longer an orphan! You've been accepted by the beloved and He has a group of people that are ready to love on you. Be receptive to their love. Know that your Heavenly Father is looking to embrace you into the Kingdom and celebrate you. He is not mad at you. He loves you and He is your Father.

PART 3

Moving Beyond Betrayal to Freedom

So how do we move beyond the betrayal to freedom?

Renewing Your Mind

I believe, in order to move beyond the betrayal, we must renew our minds and forget the things of old.

- When old thoughts about the situation or the person try to creep back up, confront those thoughts by speaking the word of God to it.

- Begin to focus on your new destination that God has for you.

- Use your imagination to see yourself in new relationships, new places and doing new things

- Be Discerning

- Pay attention to red flags or warnings that the Holy Spirit will give you concerning the person or situation

- When you have made the decision to move forward or after you've gone through your healing process, that person or situation may try to resurface. God can repair and turn around any situation that was broken, but this is something that you have to be very sensitive to. If you discern ulterior motives, then don't entertain it. If you discern that they are ready to move forward then be open and restore them in the spirit of meekness.

- Allow Holy Spirit to direct you when it comes to reconciliation or starting a new relationship.

- Move to freedom

- Focus on being free and staying free. Don't feel like you need to explain yourself to move forward.

- Remember, you don't owe them anything, but to love them and they don't owe you anything.

- Move forward unapologetically. You don't need the approval or support from man to move forward and be free.

Getting Unstuck

Yes, it happened. But don't stay stuck there. Don't rehearse the issue in your mind and don't consider the things of old. When you do that, your recalling all the memories of trauma, hurt and rejection to live inside of you. God wants to do a new thing, but you will not perceive it if your still looking at your past. It's time to forget the things behind you and reach forward for the things that are before you. It's time to get moving and press forward to the high calling of God for your life.

They meant it for evil against you, but God meant it for your good. It's freeing to know that God wants to use your pain to purify you and have you come out as pure gold. When you don't allow Him to process you through your pain then you'll miss out on the grace He wants to give you to step into freedom. He wants you to count it all joy when you go through hardship, because the testing of your faith will produce patience. He wants you to exemplify the fruit of the Spirit, so you can bear much fruit. He will prune every branch to test and see if you'll still abide in Him.

True Freedom

He wants His Spirit to surround you, so you can receive the liberation from the things that have held you bound. He wants you free indeed. As you move forward from the things that have held you back, you'll have the courage to trust, hope, and love again. God can restore the years that have been eaten up by the enemy. It takes your cooperation, your willingness and your obedience to co labor with Him in walking into freedom. It's a journey that He wants to walk you in. Allow Him access to show you the way to freedom.

He is the way to freedom. When you fix your gaze on Him you will not be distracted by the things and people that will try to steal your attention. As you talk and walk with Him, He will begin to reveal Himself to you as your Friend, Mentor, Lover and Father. That will shift your mind from the sting and have you move beyond the betrayal. Let Him manifest Himself to you and build a relationship.

Now when you feel free, don't get so excited in your freedom that you use it entertain your flesh. Stay in the guidelines of scripture to use your freedom for Holiness and win those that may be lost. Do not get entangled again in the yoke of bondage you were made FREE from! Now move forward and be free, live free and love free! Christ has liberated you!

The only way this 3 part healing process to freedom will work for you, is if you're saved. Jesus is the only way, the truth and the life to heal and free you. He is the antidote from the poisonous sting of betrayal. He has the answer and He is the answer to your pain. Receive Him today and allow Him to do a great work on the inside of you. If you are not saved and would like to know Jesus as your personal Savior, you can read and repeat this prayer:

"Lord God, I come to you as a sinner seeking for salvation. Forgive me of all the sins I have committed against you. I want to be right with You. The bible says if I confess with my mouth that "Jesus is the Lord," and believe in my heart that God raised Him from the dead, I will be saved. (Romans 10:9) I believe with my heart by faith and confess with my mouth that Jesus is Lord and Savior of my life. Thank you for saving me! In Jesus Name, Amen.

Congratulations!!! You've just been grafted in as a son or daughter in the Kingdom of God! Heaven is celebrating you and Jesus is excited to start this journey with you to wholeness, freedom and love. You are now in Christ Jesus a new creature in Him, the old has passed away and now He will make ALL things NEW concerning you! (2 Corinthians 5:17-21)

76262028R00031

Made in the USA
Columbia, SC
23 September 2019